Co

STO

**ACPL ITEM
DISCARDED**

D0849550

Exploring Fields and Lots

EASY SCIENCE PROJECTS

Just beyond your doorstep is a world of living things. A field, a vacant lot, or even a small grassy spot is home to many kinds of plants and animals. How do these plants and animals live and survive in their surroundings? With the help of this book, you can find out. You'll observe, measure, compare, experiment, and record your findings. You'll think about what you find, answer questions that interest you, and come up with new questions. That's how scientists work, and you can work that way too. Use this book as a field guide when you explore out-of-doors—or just read it for pleasure.

EXPLORING FIELDS AND LOTS

EASY SCIENCE PROJECTS

By Seymour Simon

Pictures by Arabelle Wheatley

GARRARD PUBLISHING COMPANY
CHAMPAIGN, ILLINOIS

Library of Congress Cataloging in Publication Data

Simon, Seymour.
  Exploring fields and lots.

    SUMMARY: A handbook of simple projects which sends
young science detectives to explore fields and vacant
lots to observe and record their findings about plant
and animal life.
    Includes index.
    1. Biology—Field work—Juvenile literature.
2. Biology—Experiments—Juvenile literature.
[1. Biology—Experiments] I. Wheatley, Arabelle.
II. Title.
QH318.5.S55   574'.07'2   77-4477
ISBN 0-8116-6108-3

Copyright © 1978 by Seymour Simon. All rights reserved. Manufactured in the U.S.A.

€O. SCHOOLS
C862621

CONTENTS

1. You Are an Explorer

The orange and red body of a creature comes into view. Fifteen pairs of legs carry it swiftly along the ground. The long, jointed feelers on its head wave from side to side, and its poisonous claws are raised. Moving quickly, the creature seizes its struggling prey and disappears in the undergrowth.

Is this a new form of life found on Mars? Is it a creature from someone's nightmare? Or does this thing really exist on earth? The answer is that it exists on earth. You can find it in the nearest field or vacant lot.

The creature is a centipede. It is smaller than your little finger. But it is a hunter and a killer. It preys upon the insects, worms, and other small animals that live among tall grasses.

Even the smallest field or lot has many kinds of animals and plants. You can find out how they live by observing them and trying some of the experiments in this book.

You'll work the way a scientist-explorer does. You'll look and listen carefully. You'll use a thermometer to measure temperature. You'll think and you'll ask questions. You'll try to remember all the things that you find out.

But it's difficult to remember everything. You think that you'll always remember that orange and red centipede. But weeks later you find you have forgotten how many legs it had. Or perhaps you've forgotten how it captured its prey.

How can you remember such things? You can keep a notebook when you go out exploring. Many scientists keep one. They call it a journal or a log. As times goes on, you'll find that your journal becomes more and more valuable to you.

Your journal can be any sort of note-book—anything that you can write in. Your journal belongs to you. The ideas and information that you put in it are your own. You can keep it to yourself or let someone else see it, as you wish. Nobody is going to correct it or criticize it.

In your journal you can keep notes about the animals, plants, and other things you see. You can make drawings or sketches to help you remember. Take your journal along with you when you go out to explore a field or a lot. Here are some ideas to help make your journal a good one.

Write down the date and the time of day. Tell what the weather was like: clear, cloudy, rainy, or snowy. What was the temperature? Where were you? You will never regret taking too many notes. You may only regret taking too few.

If you live in a city, you can begin by exploring vacant lots or parks. In the suburbs or in the country, you can explore fields, your own backyard, or the school grounds. Whatever spot you pick, visit it often to see what's going on.

This book will help you explore the life of a small area. It will show you new ways of looking at your surroundings and thinking about them.

To be a scientist-explorer you need to know what to watch for. You need to know how to find out facts. That's what this book is really about—it explains methods that scientists use and that you can use too.

You don't need many materials for these projects. Your journal, a pen or pencil, and your curiosity are enough to get you started. Read through the book and choose the projects you would like to do. Even if you don't actually do any of them, you may enjoy reading about a small piece of the natural world that is nearly at your doorstep.

2. Little Climates

Everybody knows that Alaska's climate is different from Florida's. But few people realize that in any one grassy lot there may be a number of different climates. For example, the south slope of a hill gets more sunlight than the slope that faces north. An open area gets more sunlight and is windier than a sheltered spot. It may be windier in the tops of tall grasses than in the tangled roots close to the ground. Because water is being given off from the soil, the air right above the ground is usually damper than the air near your face.

These little climates help to explain why certain animals live in one spot rather than another. For example, centipedes, slugs, and pill bugs need dampness. They live close to the ground. These animals also need shade. They avoid the sunlight by living under plants, rocks, and rotting materials.

Many garden spiders, ladybug beetles, leaf hoppers, and other animals live higher up. You'll find them among the stems of grasses and other plants. They do very well in sunny or windy spots.

Plants, too, live in different little climates. Mosses and mushrooms are two kinds that need damp places with little direct sunlight. But dandelions, ragweed, and many kinds of grasses need lots of sunlight and not too much water. Here are some ways that you can find out more about the little climates in lots and other spots with tall grasses.

Project: Finding temperature in different little climates

You Will Need: A thermometer of the kind you might place outside your window, your journal, and a pen or pencil

Find a bare place in a lot or field. Lay the thermometer on it, making sure the bulb is touching the soil. Leave it there for a minute or two. Read the thermometer and record the temperature. Now find the temperature of the air at a level just below your knee.

Compare the two temperatures. Even though the places are only a short distance apart there may be a 10°-20° difference.

Repeat your temperature measurements in different places around the lot—by shrubs, under a tree, or in damp places. You may be surprised at the differences.

Take temperature readings on the north and south slopes of a hill or a

mound. How do the readings compare? The difference depends upon the direction in which the slope faces. Because it receives more sunlight, a south-facing slope is always warmer. If you were a warmth-loving animal, on which side of a slope would you live?

18

Which is warmer in the sunlight, dry soil or wet soil? Check your answer by taking surface temperatures of dry and wet soil at various times during the day. There are two reasons why the wet soil is cooler. One is that water takes longer to heat up than soil. The second is that as water is heated and goes off into the air as water vapor, it carries away heat.

Repeat your temperature measurements on cloudy and sunny days. Try to take temperature readings during all four seasons. If you have a chance, take the temperature under a layer of snow as well as on the surface of the snow. Snow holds in heat—it is good insulation. Soil temperatures under a layer of snow are often higher than the temperature of air that is just above the snow.

Think about how the temperatures of these little climates might affect animals and plants. For example, small plants covered by a layer of snow might survive very cold weather better than uncovered plants. Jot down any other examples that you can think of.

Project: Finding out about the winds in different places

You Will Need: Some stiff plastic sheets, a pair of scissors, two large pins, two wooden sticks, your journal, and a pen or pencil

Make two pinwheels by following the directions below. Make sure the wheels spin freely.

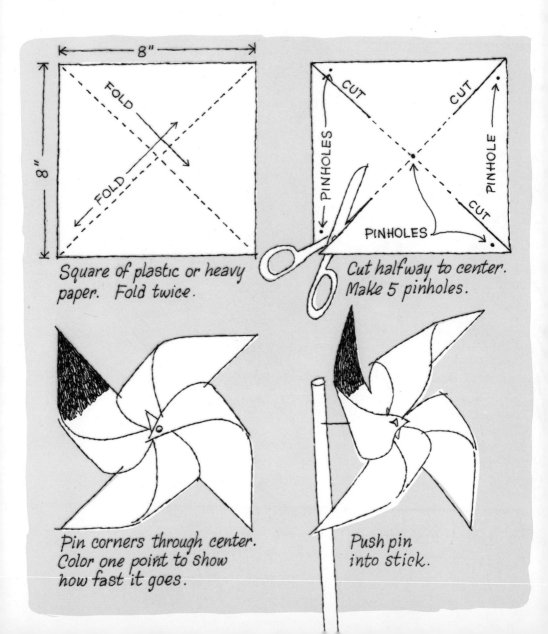

8"

8"

FOLD

FOLD

Square of plastic or heavy paper. Fold twice.

CUT

CUT

PINHOLES

PINHOLE

PINHOLES

CUT

Cut halfway to center. Make 5 pinholes.

Pin corners through center. Color one point to show how fast it goes.

Push pin into stick.

In a sunny, grassy place, put one of the pinwheels just above the ground. Hold another pinwheel at the height of the tallest grasses. Do both wheels spin at the same rate? If they spin at different rates, then one level must be breezier than the other.

Try the two pinwheels at different places, at different heights, and in shade and in sun. Record your findings in your journal.

Some plants and animals live away from the wind. Other plants and animals can live in places where winds are very strong. In even a small area there may be many little climates. And each may have its own kind of plant and animal life.

Project: How various amounts of sunlight affect plants

You Will Need: A package of plant seeds, such as beans or corn, two flower pots, soil, water, your journal, and a pen or pencil

All green plants need light in order to live and grow. They use the light to make their own food. Some kinds of plants need a lot of light. Others need much less. Look around outdoors. In some places a tree or a rock shades the ground during most of the day. The plants that grow in that shade are often different from plants growing in sunnier places.

Here's a way to find out how the sunlight in a little climate affects a plant's growth. Plant five or six seeds in each of the flower pots. Follow the planting directions on the seed packet. Place one flower pot on a sunny windowsill. Place the other pot in the same room but away from the sunlight. Keep the soil in both pots moist but not soggy.

Compare the seedlings after they have sprouted and are one week old. Count the number of leaves on each one and observe their color. Measure the height of each plant.

If the leaves do not grow, they may appear as tiny bumps on the stem. Measure the distance between the

leaves or between the bumps. Record your observations in your journal.

A taller plant with fewer leaves may not be as healthy as a shorter plant with more leaves. Which plants seem to be sturdier and healthier: the ones left in sun or the ones left in shade? Do you think the same thing would be true of other kinds of seedlings too?

Bean and other large-sized seeds contain food for young plants. The seedlings can grow for several days even without sunlight. But what do you think would happen after several weeks? Keep the two flower pots in their places and check them each week. Record your findings.

3. Finding Out about Plants

Look around at the plants that grow in a field or in a vacant lot. Use the following guide to help identify them. After you have learned how to identify a plant, search for it in other places. Do you always find it in the same kind of surroundings? What do these surroundings tell you about a plant's needs? Which kind is better able to survive over a long time: plants that need particular surroundings or plants that can grow in many different surroundings?

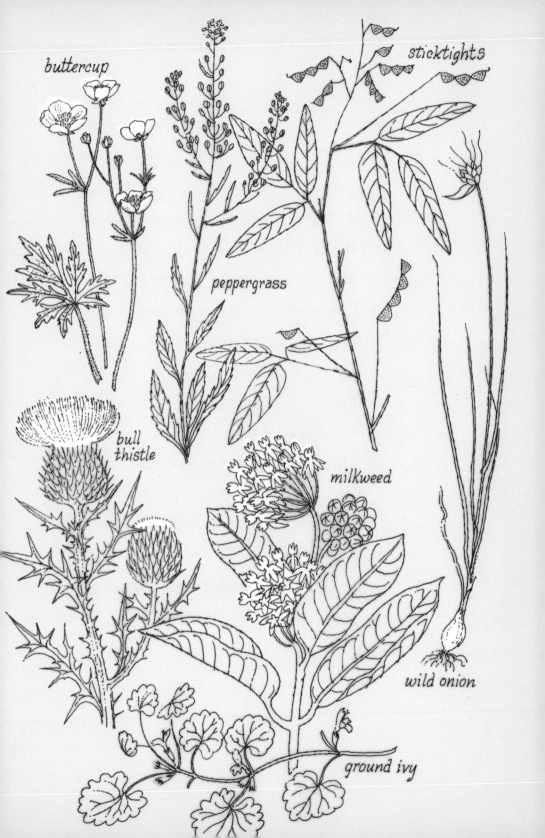

buttercup

sticktights

peppergrass

bull
thistle

milkweed

wild onion

ground ivy

Project: Identifying plants in grassy places

You Will Need: Your journal, a pen or pencil, and the following guide to grasses and other plants. A magnifying lens will be helpful in identifying them and looking at their parts

The guide may not tell you the exact name of every plant you find. But it can help you group plants with their relatives. Plants are easier to observe than animals because they don't run away.

Try to draw or photograph different plants and place their pictures in your journal.

GRASSES

It is hard to tell one kind of close-cropped lawn grass from another. But it is easy to tell if a plant belongs to the grass family. Most grasses have leaves that are long and narrow and pointed at the end. They have hollow, jointed stems. The grass family takes in plants such as corn, wheat, barley, rice, and sugar cane. Lawn grasses include bluegrass, ryegrass, Bermuda grass, crabgrass, and foxtail.

leaf blade

joint

leaf sheath

underground stem

roots

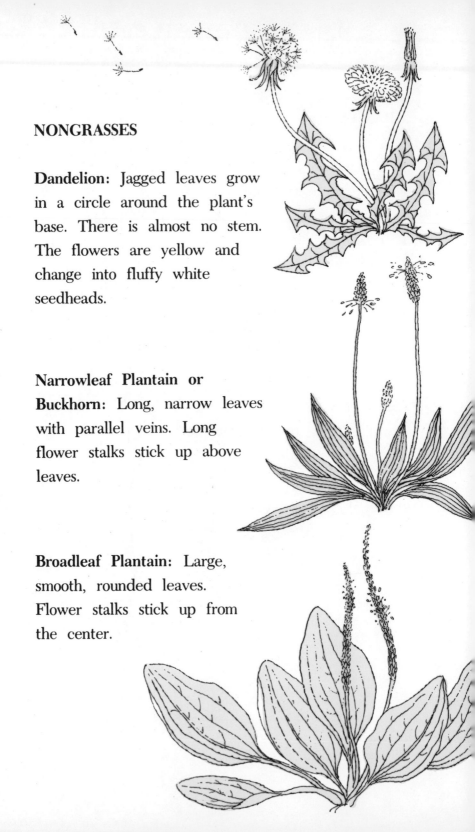

NONGRASSES

Dandelion: Jagged leaves grow in a circle around the plant's base. There is almost no stem. The flowers are yellow and change into fluffy white seedheads.

Narrowleaf Plantain or Buckhorn: Long, narrow leaves with parallel veins. Long flower stalks stick up above leaves.

Broadleaf Plantain: Large, smooth, rounded leaves. Flower stalks stick up from the center.

Great Mullein: Large leaves covered with hairs that feel velvety to the touch. Needs strong sunlight. Has a long, flower-bearing stem, which may grow to twice your height. Flowers are bright yellow.

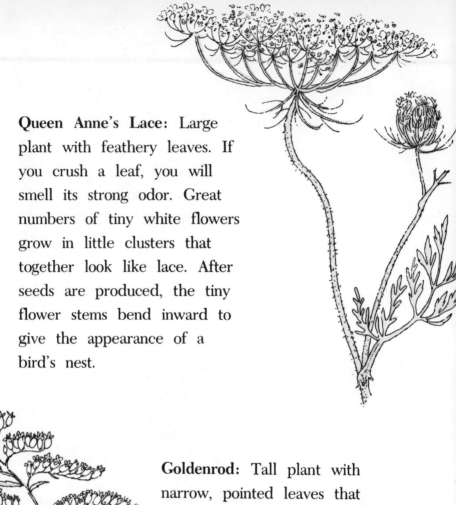

Queen Anne's Lace: Large plant with feathery leaves. If you crush a leaf, you will smell its strong odor. Great numbers of tiny white flowers grow in little clusters that together look like lace. After seeds are produced, the tiny flower stems bend inward to give the appearance of a bird's nest.

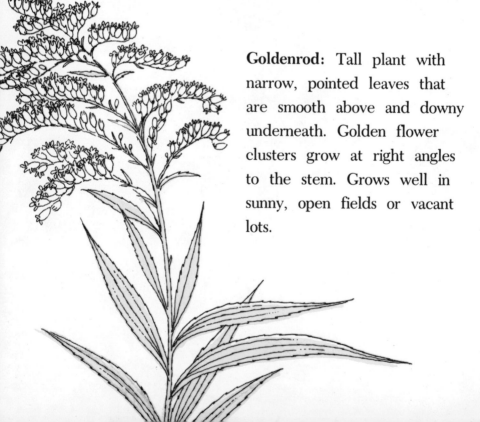

Goldenrod: Tall plant with narrow, pointed leaves that are smooth above and downy underneath. Golden flower clusters grow at right angles to the stem. Grows well in sunny, open fields or vacant lots.

Ragweed: Some kinds of ragweed are huge—they may be two or even three times your height. These large kinds have rough, hairy leaves. The smaller kinds have leaves that look lacy or feathery.
In late summer and early autumn, the pollen of these plants causes hay fever in some people.

CO. SCHOOLS
C862621

Poison Ivy: Leaves grow in groups of three. They are often shiny and toothed. In the fall, poison ivy produces clusters of whitish yellow berries. Poison ivy can grow along the ground or as a vine on trees and rocks. *Do not touch or go near this plant.*

Project: Examining the parts of plants

You Will Need: Plastic bags for collecting, pieces of tissue paper, a soft
lead pencil, wax paper, your journal,
and a pen or pencil

Pick up samples of leaves from the
ground and put them in a plastic bag
to take home. Perhaps you can sketch
or photograph some of the kinds of
leaves that you see as well as the
trees they fell from.

At home, you can preserve some of
the leaves. First place a leaf between
two pieces of wax paper or clear
plastic food wrap. Then place this
sandwich between the pages of a

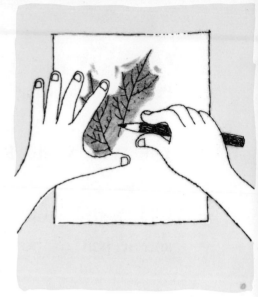

book. If the book is not heavy, put another book on top of it.

You can also make leaf rubbings at home. Place the leaf on a flat, hard surface and cover it with a sheet of tissue paper. Hold your pencil nearly parallel to the paper. Rub the lead softly back and forth over the leaf. After a few tries you should be able to make clear rubbings. Identify the

leaf prints and tape them into your journal for reference.

Back outdoors, compare the stems of short plants and tall plants. Note that tall plants need sturdier stems to support them than short plants do. Some stems are stiffened by woody material and can hold up a heavy weight.

In a vacant lot or a field (but not in a park or on a lawn), tug a few small plants out of the soil, roots and all. Look at the roots. They are the anchors of the plants. Some plants uproot easily. They are likely to be growing in damp soil or protected places. Some plants are difficult to uproot. These are likely to be growing in dry and windy spots. Their roots grow deep into the soil. They anchor the plant firmly against the wind. They enable it to take water from the soil.

Project: Finding out about plants that don't grow in soil

You Will Need: A magnifying lens, your journal, and a pen or pencil

Not all plants grow in soil. Some grow on rocks. Others grow on the trunks of trees and other plants.

Lichens are flat, grayish green plants that are often found covering the surfaces of rocks. Lichens are really made up of two different plants that help each other. One is a nongreen plant and the other is a green plant.

Break off a piece of lichen and look at it through a magnifying lens. The white or gray part that you see is a fungus. A fungus is a nongreen plant. So it cannot make its own food. It depends instead on other plants for its food. The fungus part of the lichen acts as an anchor on the rock's surface. The fungus obtains and holds

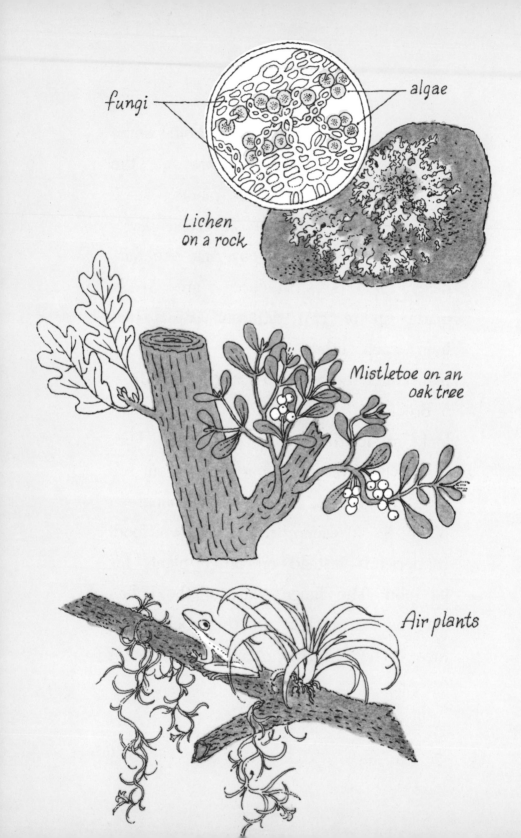

fungi

algae

Lichen
on a rock

Mistletoe on an
oak tree

Air plants

water. And it holds the green plant up to the sun.

The greenish part of a lichen is an alga. It makes food both for itself and for the fungus in which it lives. The lichen is a hardy plant that can live in many different climates.

Look for other kinds of plants that do not need soil. Some may be growing on trees or shrubs. Vines such as mistletoe send their roots into the living tree. They remove water and sap for themselves. In some regions there are plants called air plants. They also live on trees and shrubs. But they use their hosts only for support. They take what they need to make food from the air, the rain, and dust.

Look at rotting tree stumps or fallen branches for shelflike bracket funguses. Look among the branches and on the shady sides of living trees for green mosses. Look for molds of different colors growing in piles of damp, rotting leaves or on parts of dead plants. All of these are plants that can grow without soil.

Project: Setting up and caring for a grassy terrarium

You Will Need: An old aquarium tank or a clean wide-mouthed jar, plastic bags for collecting, paper towels, a bag of aquarium gravel, your journal, and a pen or pencil

Collect several kinds of grass and nongrass plants from a vacant lot or a field. Look for smaller, younger plants. These will usually do better in a terrarium. Make a note of the conditions under which you find the plants growing. Also collect some of the soil from around the plants.

Carry the plants and soil home in plastic bags that contain some wet paper towels. They will keep the plants from drying out. You may also want to collect a rock or two to make the terrarium look more natural.

For your terrarium it is a good idea to use a layer of gravel at the bottom to provide for drainage. Use the soil you collected as the top layer.

Try to set up the terrarium in the same way that you found the plants growing in the field.

Keep the terrarium in the same kind of light that the plants were getting out of doors: either direct sunlight or shade. Add water whenever the soil becomes dry, but not so much that it becomes soggy. It's best to water with a spray so that a stream of water doesn't wash the soil away.

There is a good chance that you will bring in some insects along with the plants you have collected. You may also find spiders, earthworms, or other small soil animals. Look for cocoons or egg cases on the leaves of the plants or in the soil. Check them each day to see what hatches. You may want to cover the tank with some screening to keep anything from getting out.

You can set up several different terrariums with plants that you find. A terrarium is a bit of the outdoors that you can keep indoors. With a terrarium you can easily observe the changes in the life of a grassy spot.

4. Finding Out about Animals

The plants that grow in grassy places provide food and shelter for many animals. The bigger animals, such as squirrels, are easy to spot. Smaller animals are harder to observe.

Try to be very quiet when looking for animals. Sit or stand for a few minutes without moving suddenly or making any sounds. After you begin to move around, walk slowly and carefully. You don't want to scare away insects and other small animals.

As you move around, look for clues to animals as well as for the animals themselves.

Look for movements in the grass, in the tops of trees, and in bushes. Listen for the rustling of dry leaves, the snapping of twigs, and the chirps of crickets and birds.

A web is a clue to a spider. A hole in a leaf is a clue to an insect.

Nutshells under a tree may show that squirrels have built nests in the tree's branches. Cropped grass is a sign that rabbits or other plant eaters have been around. A feather or an empty nest is a clue to a bird.

Project: Looking for animals on your hands and knees

You Will Need: A magnifying lens, small glass jars, an outdoor thermometer, your journal, and a pen or pencil

Pick a small area to explore closely. Get down on your hands and knees and begin to search slowly through the grass. A magnifying lens will help you to see small animals up close. Notice the number of legs each has. Only the small animals called insects have six legs.

Move rocks and sticks aside carefully and look underneath. You may find centipedes, millipedes, pill bugs, slugs, and snails, none of which are insects. If you roll a large rock or a log to one side, be sure to replace it when you have finished observing.

snail

slug

millipedes

pillbugs

centipede

Make a record in your journal of what you see and find. Watch to see what insects and other small animals in the grass are doing. Try to see where they are going. Do any of the animals seem to be eating? Are any of them carrying food or bits of material? Do they seem to react to such things as light or shadow or an object in their path? The longer you observe the more you notice.

Perhaps you can make a small mark that will show the place you're examining. Then you can come back to it at another time. There may be changes. The animals may change as the seasons change—a caterpillar, for instance, turns into a butterfly.

Note in your journal the time of day you see various animals. For example, you'll probably spot more birds in the early morning or early evening than in the middle of the afternoon. Note the weather, too. You may find certain animals more active just after a rain than during a dry spell. What other conditions might affect the kinds of animals you find?

Choose a different spot, one that is covered by a layer of rotting leaves and other matter. Remove the leaves layer by layer. Look for ants, termites, earthworms, spiders, and many kinds of beetles. You can better observe some of these small animals by placing them in a glass jar.

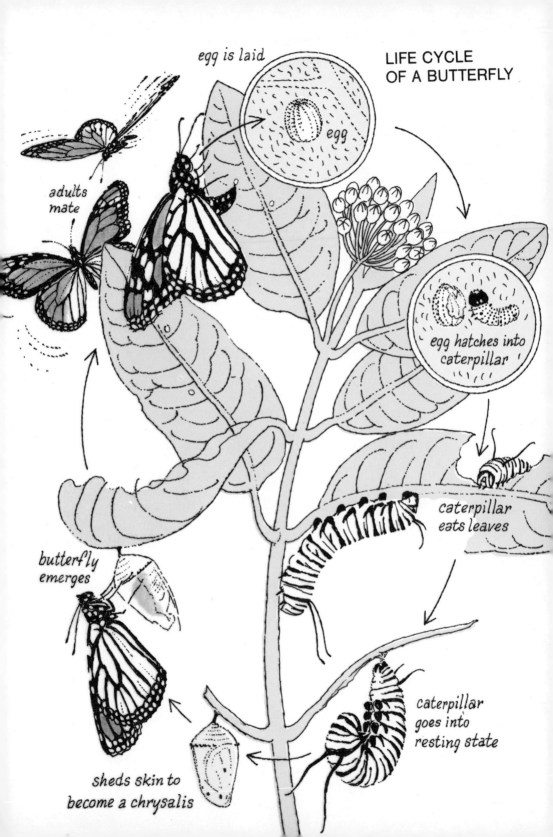

LIFE CYCLE
OF A BUTTERFLY

egg is laid

egg

adults mate

egg hatches into caterpillar

caterpillar eats leaves

butterfly emerges

caterpillar goes into resting state

sheds skin to become a chrysalis

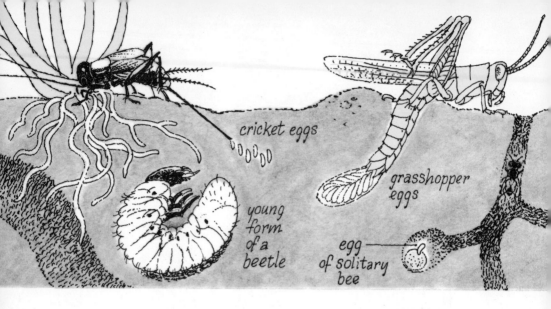

cricket eggs

grasshopper eggs

young form of a beetle

egg of solitary bee

Dig down into the soil beneath the litter. Look for tiny insect eggs and cocoons. Look for burrows and tunnels in the soil. Use your thermometer to compare the temperature at the surface with that at the bottom of the hole. Temperatures below the surface usually don't change as rapidly as air temperatures.

Next look for animals that live on the plants in a field. Look on both sides of leaves, flowers, fruits, buds, and the joints between leaves and stems. Many animals live only on plants, and you should be able to observe some of them.

Look for cocoons attached to stems and leaves of grasses. Look for caterpillars inching along stems. They often do great damage to plants. Look for partly eaten leaves and flowers, which are clues to caterpillars.

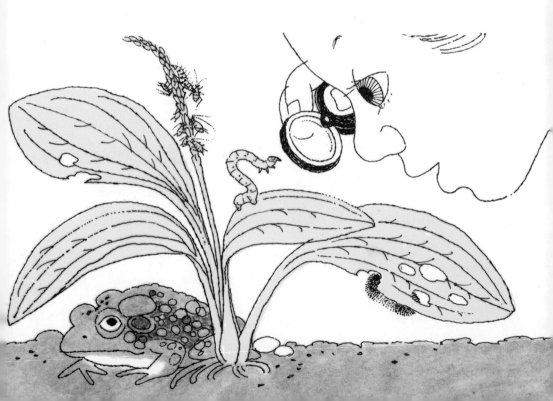

Project: Making and using an insect net

You Will Need: Cheese cloth, a wire coat hanger, a stick or broom handle, an old sheet, a needle and thread, your journal, and a pen or pencil

Make a simple insect net with some cheesecloth, a wire coat hanger, and a broom handle (see diagram). Sweep the net through the top of the grass. Twist the net closed, and then examine what you have caught.

Spread an old bed sheet on the ground, and shake the contents of the net onto it. Insects and other small animals will go hopping, flying, and

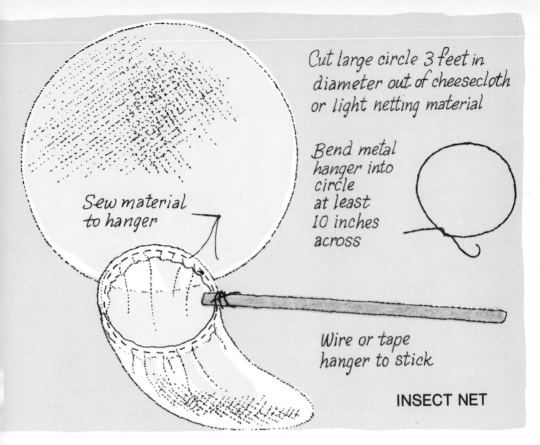

Cut large circle 3 feet in diameter out of cheesecloth or light netting material

Sew material to hanger

Bend metal hanger into circle at least 10 inches across

Wire or tape hanger to stick

INSECT NET

crawling in all directions. You can see them more easily on the sheet than on the ground. Many insects and other animals blend in well with their natural surroundings. This helps them to escape being noticed—and eaten—by their enemies.

Here are some of the kinds of insects and other small animals that you may find with a net sweep through the grass. Remember, all insects have six legs. They also have three body parts.

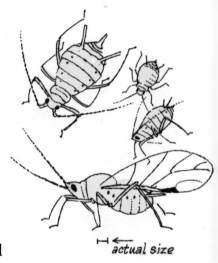

Aphids are small, soft-bodied insects that are usually green.

actual size

Ants are small, narrow-waisted insects. They may be black, red, brown, or yellow. At certain seasons you may find some ants with wings.

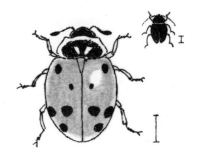

←actual size

Beetles are hard-bodied insects. They have folded wings on their backs but rarely fly. Most that you will find are smaller than your thumb.

Leaf hoppers are insects with oval-shaped bodies that may be green, black, brown, or white. They can move sideways, hop, or fly.

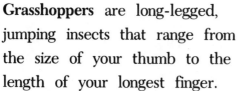

Grasshoppers are long-legged, jumping insects that range from the size of your thumb to the length of your longest finger.

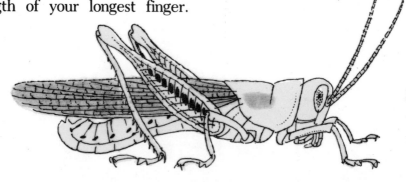

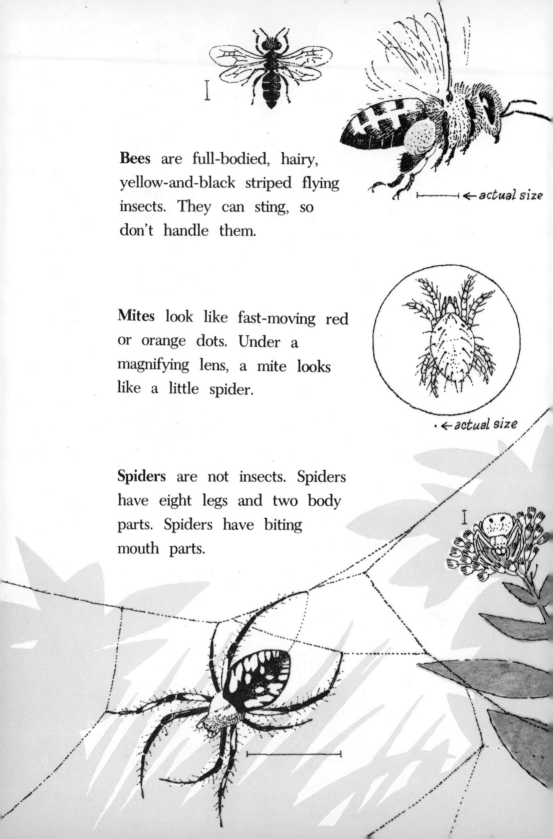

Bees are full-bodied, hairy, yellow-and-black striped flying insects. They can sting, so don't handle them.

← actual size

Mites look like fast-moving red or orange dots. Under a magnifying lens, a mite looks like a little spider.

. ← actual size

Spiders are not insects. Spiders have eight legs and two body parts. Spiders have biting mouth parts.

Keep a careful record in your journal of what you do and what you observe. As you explore, think about questions such as these. Where do animals in a field make their homes? How do animals depend on plants? In what ways are they different from one another? In what ways are they alike? Jot down other questions.

You may not know the answers to all the questions that you can think of. But the questions will help you to look at the things around you and to try to understand them. Even a great scientist doesn't know all the answers. A great scientist is more likely to know how to ask the right questions and how to search for the answers.

INDEX